HEADLINES

Essential Poets Series 318

Canada Council for the Arts
Conseil des arts du Canada

ONTARIO ARTS COUNCIL
CONSEIL DES ARTS DE L'ONTARIO

an Ontario government agency
un organisme du gouvernement de l'Ontario

Guernica Editions Inc. acknowledges the support of the Canada Council for the Arts and the Ontario Arts Council. The Ontario Arts Council is an agency of the Government of Ontario.

We acknowledge the financial support of the Government of Canada.

HEADLINES

Michael Fraser

GUERNICA
EDITIONS
TORONTO • CHICAGO • BUFFALO • LANCASTER (U.K.)
2025

Guernica Founder: Antonio D'Alfonso

Michael Mirolla, editor
David Moratto, cover and interior design

Guernica Editions Inc.
1241 Marble Rock Rd., Gananoque, (ON), Canada K7G 2V4
2250 Military Road, Tonawanda, N.Y. 14150-6000 U.S.A.
www.guernicaeditions.com

Distributors:
University of Toronto Press Distribution (UTP)
5201 Dufferin Street, Toronto (ON), Canada M3H 5T8
Independent Publishers Group (IPG)
814 N Franklin Street, Chicago, IL 60610, U.S.A.

First edition.
Printed in Canada.

Legal Deposit—Third Quarter
Library of Congress Catalogue Card Number: 2024946073
Library and Archives Canada Cataloguing in Publication
Title: Headlines / Michael Fraser.
Names: Fraser, Michael, 1969- author.
Series: Essential poets ; 318.
Description: Series statement: Essential poets series ; 318
Identifiers: Canadiana 2024045488X |
ISBN 9781771839822 (softcover)
Subjects: LCGFT: Poetry.
Classification: LCC PS8561.R2978 H43 2025 | DDC C811/.6—dc23

'Boldly going where hundreds have gone before'
does not make headlines.

—NEIL DEGRASSE TYSON

CONTENTS

TWO PHOTOGRAPHERS TURN THEIR LENSES ON BLACK CULTURE AND IDENTITY

Globe and Mail—May 12, 2022

These images exercise words out of you,
takes the loud away,
resets the internet across your face,
platters landscapes and streetscapes like
high-end dinner courses evening breezes
sieve through.
Curious how the city thins before a lens,
catches onlookers unawares,
all the moon and its white broken-plate
appearances hovering over downtown,
the skyline's phase swept into your
mind's know-how.
There are heightened afros and someone
coming between you and pieces of arcade
the 80's would be proud of.
The acapella buckets of your thought
moving away, each photo the type of
wow you'd never turn away from.

WILL SMITH SLAPS CHRIS ROCK AFTER JADA PINKETT SMITH JOKE AT OSCARS

Washington Post—Mar. 27, 2022

Thank you Chris for not biting back,
for saving us from the spectacle of two
black men wrestling like mud-rolling swine
showcased on the Oscar's world-lit stage.
Think how all the years of heroic progress
would have been whittled to a halt,
all the red-hat haters pouncing—see,
told you so, that's just who they are.
Will's action is a type of land drowning,
a continent ripping itself apart,
each scorched word fueled by a volcanic voice
lava-fast and catching up to its own sound.
You feel the burn blister through you,
your eyes camera-whipped,
and yet you pivot, keep the evening
to its pace. This is what control looks like,
all of you hugging the now,
draining the poison at its source.

OTTAWA POLICE APOLOGIZE FOR HANDLING OF INCIDENT AFTER WHITE WOMAN CALLS 911 ON BLACK MAN IN A PARK

THE GLOBE & MAIL—JULY 10, 2020

Summer keeps moving, even when I try
to hold it still. The park takes in bees
and butterflies by the eyeful. Marigolds and
lilies are pure class under this much July,
their colours flashing all I want serenity to be.
In bushes, I hear crickets get a touch of air.
Squirrels double back across the shared footpath,
their tails fluffed in full-flight fury.
All of nature serving its type of symmetry.
There's so much beauty my camera can't
frame it all in.
Then everything skids to a stop.
I can't sidestep the finger pointed at me,
or wish it back to its silence. I tell the
dispatcher what I'm about, tell her how
I shape the concept of me, while my phone
is pressed to preserve each moment
striding into the present. Look how
trees reach for the stratosphere without
thinking they did anything wrong.

SAMMY SOSA EXPLAINS WHY HIS SKIN HAS GOTTEN LIGHTER

The Spun (Sports Illustrated)—Jun. 14, 2020

It's the effect of a cream I use before
my head home-plates the pillow.
It's just how my skin mutes itself
and tunes the blanco on full-blast.
I think it brings out the thinned hue
that's always resided in my bone.
This is how aging takes my skin apart
in exiled layers. All those years running
loose under full sun.
It's how I tiptoe with spiked cleats into
the Dominican elite. They call me to
their houses now, and I don't hear
the banana bunches of circus laughter
stealing bases behind my back.
It's the way I fold more greenbacks
and set the day on stun when I backtag
my swelling bank accounts.
It's how I finally get to whack the African
clear out of me. Yes, the cream has
also made the hair straighter.
My doctor is still puzzled by that too.

CAN I BE A BLACK MOTHER IN A WORLD SO DANGEROUS TO BLACK CHILDREN?

GLOBE AND MAIL—MAY 12, 2021

Canada, these record deep-fried August
days belie the cold I know will be here,
certain as the colour blue is not red.
Certain this dry dogwood summer will be
contained by winter's flat brush, and I won't
be able to forgive you for the myths you ride.
I know my son will be reduced to a stare.
How he'll somersault round school and become
the wrong type of anything. How street
"authenticity" will chase him like a bark,
become a word he can't outrun.
I worry I always leave too much to chance,
and won't be there for him, especially
when I'm barely here for myself.
There's a lot to be said about forgetting.
You have perfected this like a shush.
I stroll out into your cooling night hug,
see how a child fills everything between
each parent's palm, her outstretched hands
tethered between now and forever,
the sky light-chipped with stars.
I kneel down to tie my shoelace
and feel the grass shudder.

'THOSE FAMILIES ARE STILL HERE': GROUP PUSHES TO COMMEMORATE FORGOTTEN BLACK NEIGHBOURHOOD IN CHARLOTTETOWN

THE GLOBE AND MAIL—FEBRUARY 25, 2021

There will always be overlooked places,
lives lifted off yesterday's shelf, and scribbled
over like years graffitied on worn wind-shredded
lap siding, baked weatherboard the thought
behind what the sun is doing.
You can still feel July thicken round the hewed
tear-drop pond, the only relic making its last stand
against erasure. Imagine the hand-built,
frayed, scrap-wood houses, and shoeless
little tackers in a watering hole which held them
the way colored clothespins hold summer on a line.
Envision the families knit together, labourers knowing
times would not close if their eyes clung to the work-hour's
lash clawing each other's backs.
How maples salt-licked the maritime air when
the day struggled to keep its weight, their poverty
kneed by winter. Remember to carry these images as
the dusk clears. Even under lamplight, the street is
shaken by shadows.

REBECCA CARROLL GREW UP THE ONLY BLACK PERSON IN HER NEW HAMPSHIRE COMMUNITY. IT TOOK HER A LONG TIME TO WRITE ABOUT THAT 'ERASURE'

Brampton Guardian—Feb. 5, 2021

Gnawed and wind-fumbled into
winter's grip, her eyes blossom
out to the rink making hairline
scribbles, oblivious to the stares
she centers, the end of her red mitts
outstretched and swinging, how her
breath shovels air beneath her hairbow.

Her life looks like a wire fence.
The way people approach like deer,
sniff, nuzzle noses in her face,
their thoughts ready to jump past her
for a handful of plump green leaves,
the way they look through her.

She's a window-full house where
people chin-by knocking, and fewer
crack-in an entrée, the way they
never slide their kicks off, plant feet
on the living room furniture and rebound
to the warm mudroom before a prompt
departure. The many rooms of her poetry
they refuse to enter.

'IN MASAI WE TRUST.' HOW THE RAPTORS' BOSS BECAME TORONTO'S MOST INFLUENTIAL SPORTS EXECUTIVE

TORONTO STAR—AUG. 21, 2021

First, become a soul born in England seeded
from two distant parts of Africa.
Then relocate to Nigeria and take in more
than the bounty in your father's language.
Become the beginning for others, and ride
your crippled boyhood friend out into the world,
the whoosh and speed he feels sitting on your
handlebars is the universe expanding.
Learn how shooting a basketball is a form of living.
Read the court by the eyeful.
Make each day on rectangles slicked with sweat,
your hands like fly-swatters pouncing after swift
backboard rebounds hurtling away like comets.
Dream of winning championships with
razzle-dazzle buzzer-beater throws.
Become a scout on your own dime and scour
a skeptical planet responding with silence.
Tell timid players to be more aggressive,
no one just gives away space, you must carve
your own lane. This is how the world works.
Become a CEO and see your thoughts enacted
in other people.

Be like a parent who only sees glory in their children,
even when they're in quicksand-losing streaks.
Effect trades to move the right pieces into place,
know how a single phone call will shatter even
the tallest men.
Embrace a city and be the centre of the word
happening, so even a sparse, vast, northern nation
will finally believe in itself.

'MY RESPONSIBILITY': TRACING THE GRAVES OF EARLY BLACK SETTLERS IN CANADA

THE GUARDIAN—JUN. 12, 2022

Because they struggled through
        winter's illness-inducing bite,
and the mouth-clenched growl from
others who wished them dead,
the face-spit and chest-punch whack
of failed crops on feeble land,
I take all the day, watch radar penetrate
and beep waves through time, see how it
        uncovers headstones, carries
        bone heaps into the present, brings
a buried keepsake into the now.
I shake each unveiling with pride,
        sweat-print my mug with wonder.
        Picks, shovels, and digging bars
        are just the beginning, each a key
        opening closed lives. I place
        marker flags on pebbled ground,
        and feel the silence breaking
across my skin.

VACCINE HESITANCY IN THE BLACK COMMUNITY IS DEEPLY ROOTED IN A HISTORYOF RACISM. OVERCOMING THAT LACK OF TRUST WILL BE A TOUGH TASK

TORONTO STAR—FEB. 6, 2021

It's because they said blacks feel pain differently.
Because depriving plantation babies of nutrition was easy.
Because sharecroppers were watched and charted like
seasons of wheat while syphilis rot barked deep into their
cells like relentless boll weevils sucking each day's blood.
Because they said we weren't human.
Because even hatred knows evil is never right.
Because modern gynie was birthed from slave women
drowning in the pit of bloodcloth-soaked labours.
Because digging graves was cheap.
Because the earth knows how to keep secrets.
Because letting your teeth blight meant nothing
to the owner who raped you daily.
Because they couldn't find enough white volunteers for
the experiment.
Because pickling a child's brain with booze was easy.
Because there are many ways to ignore someone.
Because they did everything to turn us into silence.

AKIM ALIU TO RELEASE GRAPHIC NOVEL MEMOIR TELLING HOW HE FOUND HIS VOICE TO CONFRONT RACISM IN HOCKEY

THE GLOBE AND MAIL—MAY 5, 2022

He lives in the   space
between
numbers.

Three,
the weight of languages that parade
fluently when he opens
                        his mouth to thought,
easily unlocks the Cyrillic alphabet
like a pro called up
for the big show,
knows all the meaning
English can't convey.

Seven,
the number of teeth
sucker-slapped
from his gums by a
wood-heavy fibreglass
hockey stick,
a present from his future-star teammate,
two years
his senior,
a bully cross-checking

newbies into hazed
penalty boxes,
shoving
          them face-down into
the world's beetle dung.

Four,
the years he cascaded
                    through the NHL where
                    rumours billowed like
                    thunderheads, flashing
                    lightning that burned
and charred boards
and change rooms
          smoldering around him.

BLACK SETTLERS HELPED SHAPE WESTERN CANADA

Edmonton Journal—Feb. 5, 2021

Since winter speeds in like an unloaded
        souped-up freight train, they hurry
late summer's tail through wheat fields.
Inflated with rushing clouds, the wide sky
swings like a steel door hinge,
locks away the afternoon sun.
        Dogs chase pocket gophers
and thick-furred squirrels into
ground hollows.
Death is an empty larder ahead of
        early season snows,
        the absence of hogs
        curing in the smokehouse.
A laggard hand moping through furrows
is the quickest ticket to hell.
The school is emptied till the cropping
is full and done.
Frost will settle in,
                hang the living crops,
then feast along the windowpane.

LIL UZI VERT REVEALS HE'S BLEACHING HIS SKIN

VIBE.COM—FEB. 3, 2022

This is how he unboxes himself
when everyone is looking, and takes
apart his own sound on social media,
the various forms of himself collecting
in images. He tries to return to his memory,
persistent like farm animals indenting
across a field. He continues to take his
skin beyond the town, orders it to a type
of forgetfulness, tilts his colour towards
amnesia, tells everyone to forget his past,
a narrative disordered and muddled,
still unopened to any mouth and ear.
Onlookers wonder where his name should
go when the bulk of his conscience empties.

MONTREAL'S FELIX AUGER-ALIASSIME WINS FIRST EVER TENNIS TOURNAMENT IN ROTTERDAM

MONTREAL.CTVNEWS.CA—FEB. 13, 2022

When I was four, I feared the distance
of astonishment between the baseline
and the looming net, far too much green
space for any toddler to fill.
I played all childhood, my bones mastering
the solo court playbook faster than jazz hands
waking up a neglected piano.
I was echoing promise and tuned each match
to a gift, an offering I always gave myself.
I made tennis my third language, and watched
the ocean-blue fleur-de-lis follow me like a
proud shadow, like a wave pinned to my side.
I'm becoming another's eyes, see myself opening
on a large screen, sweating my introduction
where my voice eddies in the stands.
I toss moons and suns into the air, then level
them with my racket's face, slice the angle to backspin.
I step out on courts French-kissed with summer,
feel heat heaving the horizon on red clay, plant
my feet steady on the baseline before I serve.
A let is the absence of time till the ball bounces.

TO SAVE BLACK LOYALIST BURIAL GROUNDS FROM NEGLECT, NEW BRUNSWICKERS DIG INTO THEIR SEGREGATED PAST

THE GLOBE AND MAIL—MAR. 31, 2021

A shovel represents no danger
to the ground, especially when its rusted
tip is the quickest way to rewrite history.
They dig the morning into abbreviations,
        each layer of earth a time unopened,
a piece of mid-century
handed to the day's loosening.
This is how they clear the calendar with
        a simple turn of dirt. The dust
        rises, locks stories in dry throats.
An escaped slave arrives, his tail green
as a picked switch. The soil speaks through
        his silence, his tomb shaking the
present, the noise louder than a large
murder of crows.
They picture his old eating house,
        all the brown-toned folk gathered,
        their world abased and limited,
        the hours a hatchway gate they
        couldn't open.

QUEBEC POLICE INVESTIGATING VIOLENT ARREST INVOLVING BLACK TEENAGERS AFTER VIDEO EMERGES

The Globe and Mail—Nov. 28, 2021

and no one is coming through
the red days, the blue days, the days

cupped in haze, the days laid on
their sides like oakwood-heavy

ladders leaned against a house,
the days where all you wanted

was a break, a moment to inherit
silence, feel its peace handhold

your skin in the wet-kiss burst of
humid air, and no one is coming to

say hold on, or wait, he's only 13,
you're making a mistake, let me

straighten this out like rail lines
slicing through flat prairie fields,

or this can all be explained simple
as the shape of a maple leaf, and no

one is coming to provide a habitat of
space to take-in the sidewalk's persistence

or feel how the air kicks back as it trips
down the street and crossfades, no, there

are only people with cell phone cameras,
an audience taken through extremes.

SUBBAN ENCOURAGES TEEN FACING RACISM

The News and Observer—Jan. 9, 2019

The hard, shaved-ice rink still
as a postcard background, if you
like how the Zamboni humbles
after a few sweeps, how the water
reflects like a mirror.

I can tell you I experienced all
of this before: the name-call intervals
breaking out from stands, and rebounding
off boards, the extra strong blueline push,
how they try to goad you into the penalty
box, the glue placed in my childhood gloves.

Look past the fields when you drive to the
rink. Take in the scenery like a wish.
Then continue on and rename the arena
after yourself. Know you are greater than any
one game. Know you are more than
anything they can do to you.

THE WEEKND SAYS HE'S STILL BOYCOTTING THE GRAMMYS DESPITE RULE CHANGES

BBC—May 4, 2021

Often, the notes don't know whether to
stay in genre or expand outward, find a
groove filled with new sensation, a jam

pulsed to a backbeat, a deep cut budding
out in walking basslines, anywhere intense
feeling gathers in a quiver. The way half-

notes stretch themselves, sprinkle across
sheet music like summer hailstorms, popping
the ground heavy with percussive rhythm.

The way different vibes burst open, swallow
willing listeners with the easiest gulp, effort-
less like water plummeting off mountains.

How they fall sheer through the slightest cracks,
smudge lines pencil-drawn between roots music
and its African and Appalachian children.

How it's one family is always there, holding
onto the background like an x-ray of a human
heart no one can tell is black or white.

THREE BOYS ARRESTED AFTER PELLET GUN SHOOTINGS MONDAY

Toronto Star—May 31, 2022

I was there, before it all unravelled,
moments ahead of Chaos replacing the
parking lot's calm with a bottomless chasm,
a void always returning to time's dawn.
I drove off leagues before the melee,
how car wheels carried me off to my main
life, sliced an hour in half, to get my kids
from their after-school music program.
I had no clue of the violence that occupied
the vicinity where I had ambled to my car,
where students sat on cracked stone steps,
immersed in their teenage now, and others
pretended they were Premier League potential
screening skills on the sun-washed soccer field.
I wonder what would have cropped up had I left
later and centred the lot's universe like an accident,
who knows what Chaos would have wrought,
and if my kids would have been left waiting,
their lives altered to a tremor.

TRUDEAU GREETS CROWDS AT JUNIOR CARNIVAL PARADE IN SCARBOROUGH

CBC News—Jul. 16, 2022

The children are decked like hummingbirds,
flapping their glossy slick hinges, their arms
are coloured sticky tag notes and tinselled

like the world leading up to Christmas.
Trudeau sets the mic on blast, gathers their
voices the way he did back in his teaching

days, no detail of praise too small to hatch.
Then they take his place with movement.
How their feet pitter-patter, pirouette, shuffle-

step across the day's ledge, the music blare
announcing itself from banked speaker lines,
the grains of sound overtaking the bandshell

space like blue-white hydrangea blossoms,
their sparkle-filled headdresses the feather-
flash line-drive dazzling the judges' burrow.

CAN RACISM CAUSE SCHIZOPHRENIA?

The Globe & Mail—July 12, 2021

Only if your senses were assaulted by
the steady police-shooting parades of
people caught in their daily selves,
including children being nothing but
the energy powering playground parks,
then you gandered at the full moon's
curves and knew it looked a little sideways.
Not if you can still your breathing
during your second pullover this year,
or forgive the centuries of rape tattooed
throughout your skin like a single-shade
mural, or let go of all eyes at work just
waiting for a pratfall, anything against
the narrative saying you belong.
Only if you believe the thrum of bootstraps
is a plastic metaphor you've been trying
to outclimb for years, if you've noticed most
garbage men are black, their skin cracking from
the torrid heat and bone-chill cold chorus.
It touches obvious so even four-year-olds know.
Hard work is never a type of abstract.
If you fall back in sleep, but awake a half-
hour earlier than everyone else, your mind
caught in troubles, the headaches jackhammer-
ing decades of mean through your skull.
If your heart pulses with a twang every time

you leave a store worried the alarm will
throw a tantrum, or you don't belong in
certain eatery chairs, hosting at the VIP lounge,
steering a lipstick-red Porsche, opening your
bougie front door, stepping magazine streets,
the houses gathered in adjectives, in your
upscale clothes, your own damn feet, or all the
other places no one wants you to call home.

BLACK NOVA SCOTIA LIBERAL CANDIDATE UNDETERRED AFTER CAMPAIGN SIGN BURNED

Canadian Press—July 26, 2021

Sometimes, the signs are the easiest part of
this election. They're the coloured poker chips
everyone can see stacked clear cross a table.

My caramel face is painting Truro red in all
directions, and I don't even have to personally
hammer them all into lazy summer lawns.
They multiply across front yards with smiles,
porch belly-laughs, and trainloads of
reassuring answers.
My confidence is a circle widening
with each smooth, masked encounter.
This is what accomplishment feels like.

Then the midnight fires knock us back
into history.

I answer reporters in the voice of my ancestors.
I knock on doors, fist-bump the humid air.
I step forward holding the courage of every
young black child spreading hope within me.

ANTI-BLACK RACISM HOVERS JUST BENEATH THE SURFACE

Toronto.com—Mar. 7, 2022

It licks your face after midnight
and won't let you snooze. It shares the
bed no matter how many times you
try to push it away. It sucks milk from
its ever-giving dam, shreds its toys
like a machine, claws furniture to
practice its deep-line signature,
frays the Persian rug and pees in
the embroidered center, always lets
you know you are on its territory.
Racism shits outside the litter box,
vomits on your new shoes before
you step out the house. Its durable
lingering odour a staple pinned in the air.
It pretends to ignore you when you're
looking, then pounces with your
back turned to the day, swipes at
your head like a growling back-hoe.
You ponder its confidence, know if you
keel over now, in a few rigor mortis hours
it will eat you to the bone. Racism
becomes felid and feral like a wandering
moon when it takes off at night, joins
the shrieking back alley clowder, lets
you know no matter how tight you shut
the window, or how far away you go,
it's never out of earshot.

BLACK ALIENATION IN ACADEMIC LIFE BEGINS IN HIGH SCHOOL: STUDY

New Canadian Media—May 9, 2022

This marks where he went wrong
funneling himself to in-talk and
the settling touch of full fist-bumps,
and the fete's alley weight darkening
around them.

Girls shake and twerk past their horizon.
How he wants to jam with his round
booty-betty, the one he always eyes
from the safety of margins,
but she's upping the older guys.

He remembers his childhood unmoored,
the way he held onto astronomy.
How his eyes raked celestial skies
dusting his sleeping hours. Even now,
he feels he can tease the Big Dipper's
tail, despite the music's bone.

He knows it all centers on authenticity,
but doesn't recall the moment his ship
cleaved to the sandbank. One year
heaved on science and the rainbows fueling
books, then cool mirrored in.

CANADA'S SCREEN WORLD "DECADES BEHIND" ON BLACK REPRESENTATION, SAY INDUSTRY MEMBERS

Toronto Star—Feb. 18, 2021

First, they left us out of film reels,
glossed magazines, and posters,
anywhere a cool image could talk.

We were reserved to newspaper covers
where a criminal's picture always moved
beyond its loudness, shook its money
maker when pinned to page one.

Then we were hauled-in like fish from
the forgotten continental shelf and black-
        faced ourselves. How Huggy Bear
        juddered like paint cans in the paint
        mixer machine, his lips buzzing
        circles through Starsky and Hutch.

Then we questioned our café authenticity
when the Cosby Show threw down an
        M.D. and a J.D., all the shingled
        abbreviations we tripped over,
        false signboards of a future calm.

Now, we move in a story that deserves
better. What sets up in the eye is always
lacking, it's a pause where the
description can't be filled in, a
place where answers show up
belatedly dressed, the way a
world hints at its incompleteness.

ETOBICOKE TEEN'S BLACK HISTORY MONTH EFFORTS GET NOTICED BY ONTARIO'S LIEUTENANT GOVERNOR

Toronto.com—Feb. 26, 2021

She could have kept to what's expected:
rehash an African fashion show, re-enact
Rosa Parks sticking to her seat like cement,
even better, switch-in Viola Davis for Can con,
but she stuck to difference, befriended the change
circling around her.
How she moved everyone without friction,
the way they all flew and allowed the audience
to sit thrilled in gravity, the school hour moving
faster than a whisk. She checks the student-filled
stage, sees her mind in action, how broad-cupped
headphones crown her head. She is alight with
these experiences that pull her in.
The way she trusts the sound of her own music.

FIVE PEI MINOR HOCKEY PLAYERS SUSPENDED OVER RACIAL SLURS TOWARD N.S. PLAYER

THE GLOBE AND MAIL—FEB. 11, 2022

His head still takes on dreams
where the ice is another life,

an intersection without cars, where
players move like chess pieces,

his arms quicken like eyes, speaking
against the boards, meeting the guard-

rails most skaters call home. He hears
the din of the crowd's roar slope like

a waterfall spilling over the stands,
when the word nigger comes out of exile,

how it bursts into years and installs
itself through the stands like malware,

transferring these encounters not just to
words, but the keyhole of experience,

closing the joy in the game he loves,
leaving the rink door locked and bolted.

FOR BLACK CANADIANS, THERE'S NO GOING BACK TO THE WAY THINGS WERE

The Globe and Mail—Feb 4, 2022

No, no going back to the off-script
comments scratched across childhood
skin, the branded words bouncing like
millions of tennis balls off classroom
cinderblock walls when everyone's mind
should be cupped in images, the space quiet
with reading. No, no going back to years devoid
of summer cheer, where we watched others
enjoy pools baked in the smiling bandwidth
of cooling water, or drink from the same
fountain, and lord, the bathrooms! You know,
the ones no one cleaned because we had
to use them. No, no going back to professional
programs that lost your application or
flat-out sent you away like a dog waiting
for a drop of anything to fall off the table.
No going back to freeways laid down the
middle of our neighbourhoods like pool cues,
or bringing in growling bulldozers to tidal-
wave Africville and pull it from memory
the way farmers yank weeds from the only
ground they've ever known. No, no going
back to the heartburn of different rents,
the lost houses in bidding wars, all the
undisclosed bids thrown on a compost

heap, their obituaries disappearing into
the quicksand of boundaries. No, no
going back to the wiretap feeling while
driving anywhere and nowhere, the heart-
skip of just sitting in your car, your life
rustling like paper, your children the
ultimate screen shot, until the cops
arrived and leveled you out like a line,
and how you always resembled an event
straight from the air, the way you'd
ball-up awaiting the coming burn.

HOW TO FIX ANTI-BLACK RACISM INGRAINED IN THE TTC

Toronto Star—Jul. 5, 2020

Glide onto the subway car
before it begins to side-pelt

and skip-flow through
the earth's hollowed belly.
Feel the continent's
rocky groove shudder-shake
as steel wheels grind the
subterranean silence away.

Forget you and one other
shaded brotha were the only
ones asked to confirm your
paper transfer.

Squeeze the railing tight
like a polished clamp
as if it's an outstretched hand
a vertical thinned bridge
soldering ceiling and floor
together as the train tremors
shaking the passage shaft,
your glass reflection shot
like an unlit fuse.

AT LEAST 18 CHILDREN WERE HOSPITALIZED AND 5 PEOPLE DIED AFTER AN SUV CRASHED INTO THE WAUKESHA CHRISTMAS PARADE

CNN—Nov. 22, 2021

Please don't be black. Please don't be black. Please don't be black. Please, please, please, don't be black. Please, please don't be black. Please, please, please don't be black. Please don't be black! Please don't be black! Please, please, please, please, don't be black! Please! Don't be black. Please, please, don't be black. Please don't be black. Please don't be Please, be anything other than deep mocha-shaded, catchy caramel, umber brown, smooth gingerbread, matte tortilla, pinched penny, dark maple, honed hickory, rolling peanut, ground coffee, cinnamon bark, brunette carob, broad-rooted chocolate, sunset-shadow oak, crust-brown mahogany, and brewed morning espresso. be black! Please don't be black! Pleasssssssse! Don't be black! Please don't be black. Please don't be black! Please don't be black! Please don't be black! Please, pleeeeeeease don't be black! PLEASE, DON'T BE black!!!!!!!!

MARTHA STEWART SAYS THAT EVERYBODY SNOOP DOGG SEES AT PARTIES 'WANTS TO KNOW HOW'S MARTHA'

People—Jun. 16, 2022

Questions flicker and swell into
the offering of set lights polishing
a front-lit stage.

How Snoop's cornrow-tightened
head towers feet above her wheat-
blonde locks, the endless laughter
beam-booming between them.

This is what chemistry looks like.
Everyone knows it when they see it.
How the studio audience lathers
themselves with it, sets it tingling
along their warm clapping palms.

If it can manifest itself here, it can
humble itself anywhere.
Imagine an entire planet written
together on the same page.

ONE PERSON DEAD AFTER SHOOTING AT FUNERAL FOR TORONTO HOMICIDE VICTIM

TORONTO.CTVNEWS.CA—AUG. 12, 2022

Unknowingly, mourners wait for the ending
to come, not once but twice,
death is a calling card, a location
caught both underfoot and speeding
towards them. Tears wail and rip
into summer's fruit-filled core the way
blight spills through the hardiest of crops.
How every life is abridged and clipped,
    becomes a leaf losing its colour
    raw in the day, wind-lifted off
    a maple branch. The way we
    all eventually return to ground,
the way silence is the loudest sound.

BIAS BEHIND BARS: A GLOBE INVESTIGATION FINDS A PRISON SYSTEM STACKED AGAINST BLACK AND INDIGENOUS INMATES

GLOBE AND MAIL—NOV 11, 2020

What I did to save my neighbour
is the full-time matinee horror show
reeling through my charged mind.
A knife is almost the worst kind of language.
Its vowels remain silent until they strike.
The last images are simply red against snow.

Behind these cinder block walls is where
crimes meet, and every story takes its time
to unravel. No one arrives without bad
decisions in this reinforced-concrete box
made of time.

Every morning, someone is reaching into
the sound of his own throat. Someone is
screaming through sleep.
Every morning, I savor what I can from routine,
find joy in how mint toothpaste coats my breath,
watch the spider design its web, take in whatever
signs I can to make myself whole.

I thought Sammy was going to stay longer.
I wish him luck with fist-pumps before I walk
the three-cedar courtyard.
Again, the sky itches with rain.
I snub out the cigarette and pull smoke
through my rusted teeth.

COMEDY SERIES NEXT STOP OFFERS A SNAPSHOT OF BLACK LIFE IN TORONTO

The Globe and Mail—Sept. 30, 2020

The comedian stands on a frigid stage quiet
as an iceberg, looks out at the fallow field
of faces and begins to deepen into his own

type of global warming as he reads the audience
like tea leaves and sets himself to center the night's
existence. He's an alchemist who summons the id

and reintroduces his unchained ego as it thickens past
previous nights' gains and swells beyond his margins.
He is taking them in with sound, each punchline runs

its own lap, waves like whooping west wind through
wide-plain wheat grass. He loves the thunder punching
out of handclaps, so much power following a simple pause.

DO BLACK LIVES MATTER TO TORONTO'S GANGS?

Calgary Sun—Sep. 17, 2020

So sure of themselves when they graffiti
and knot stairwell walls with skunk weed,
how nebulas circle out their laughing mouths,
the raw profanity spill broadening,
even as moms try to baby-carriage past
the red-blue-yellow playground.
This is how they skip to results,
fall unpopular with the neighbourhood,
each resident a type of fear muting its own light.
The clear hinged take-out container messes
they splash everywhere, a type of impromptu
art the streetscape advances.
How they become untitled as the swings
they commandeer, ignore the sprouting
number of kids the years cut down.
Even toddlers can make a stray bullet become
more than a simple fact.
See the noticeable lack of sky above the monkey bars,
how it enhances their silhouettes like a presence.
The sleeves of night they put their hands on.

HEALTH CARE RESEARCHERS NEED TO ASK, 'WHO IS BLACK?' UNIVERSITY OF OTTAWA PROFESSOR SAYS

OTTAWA CITIZEN—JUL. 23, 2022

He says the gathering of ailments is crooked
and defined by numbers of junk spilling
from everyone's mouth. Each person notes
their own shift into sickness, unaware death's
progression is not unique, and will join them
eventually whether they welcome him or not.
He says how people define themselves is a
type of memory reassembled, the physical
asking itself to become a landscape where
one word is a flag planted on the margins,
the boundaries disjointed and sumo-wrestler
fastened, tidal-locked to the sure thought of one's
closed identity, the secrecy held within each
person not wanting to join the breakout decrees
without a talented dictionary present like a lawyer.

MARKING THE SECOND ANNUAL BLACK SHIRT DAY IN B.C.

CITYNEWS.CA—JAN. 14, 2022

I kept an unseen shield, put the world on pause
when it came at me crazed with screens, I looked
away and unfolded the plot,
sent the images packing.

I kept an unseen shield, tried to stay in my frame
clear my lane, when the names found me
simple on playgrounds. The sound of its quirk
finalizing the classroom lesson.

I kept an unseen shield, ready to go against
seasons locked and loaded against me,
unable to see how red the light would be,
unaware the stage floor had broken.

PERSPECTIVE: WHERE HAVE ALL THE GOOD MEN GONE?

DESERET NEWS—JUN. 20, 2022

He has so much going for him
that the day banks its own truth:
holds a physics PhD, the army stint
discharged with honours,
a square chiselled jawbone any
superhero would demand as
prerequisite, cool threads hugging
his fit bod, everything in alignment
except for the slight line-wobble
beneath average height.

He moves through the speed-dating
tables like wildfire, mirrors the tidal
wave warmth and fluffed-up thrill
they colour-match and split-screen
at him, tries to ignore the half smiles
and the lost distant postcard feeling
when he stands and goes in for the hug,
the universe of hope at speed-boost
dwindling within him.

THESE ARE 27 PEOPLE TORONTO STREETS SHOULD BE NAMED AFTER—FROM MARY ANN SHADD TO DUDLEY LAWS

Toronto Star—Jul. 1, 2020

Sometimes the city can't rise
into its biography without slip-ups,

tear-downs, and sharp uncouplings
from its claystone-footprint history.

This is how it rebrands space and takes
the dash away. Toronto, sometimes you

leave no room for me, and when I see how
night skies greet this significant skyline,

I am humbled to a fault. I watch lights
rappel down the CN Tower's lean glass face

and see them rebound up again. Then there's
the way summer storms billow, line-up, and

chase through downtown, circling in overlaps,
the streetscape caught weighted under cold-

lake rain blankets. You wonder what's in a
label as more cranes rise to swing their pelican

necks over heads moving ant-like below. Ask
the university as it turns away sideways from

its once-hidden past. Remember, a name always
gives us everything it has.

TORONTONIAN AT CENTRE OF RACIAL INCIDENT IN SOCCER SPEAKS OUT: 'I JUST STARTED THROWING UP'

Toronto Sun—Aug. 6, 2022

The N-word is more than a term,
more than a sound or idiom banged
out to hard-lengthen the longest day.
It puts you on the brink, sets the fringe
line margin, attacks you from your
blind spot, always comes in from some-
where off the road map, off-the-cuff,
never keeps its powder dry, jumps in
from low bleachers and high stands
ready to rub its scrub-brush fist against
your face, it goes in feet first for the
hard tackle, upshifts its speed when
on your trail, plays like a winger who
passes insults instead of the ball, head-
buts you close to the goal-line, drives
you offside with a push, drills down on
your weak side, knows myriad ways to
make you cry like a kid, tells you you're
shit, makes monkey sounds and throws
bananas behind the goal net, keeps you
constantly on your toes, even after the
whistle has blown.

TORONTO'S GANG CRISIS & THE RACISM OF LOW EXPECTATIONS

CNN.com—Mar. 24, 2022

The Civic snarls at midnight
sucks borrowed streetlight along
its hard-top roof, gathers neon down
its off-white meridian.

The five inside cut melodic to
beating-bust bass, their eyes red
to the wet chase tracing their lips.
One pulls his strap and tightens
to quell the guns ripening hunger.

They spot their rivals in the park's
pencil-crayoned parking lot's neck,
liming their fill of themselves.

Windows sleeve down for the
rat-a-tat-tat burst cracking the night
air open like high heat popcorn.
The boys run scattershot in unison,
try their best to speed-feet away.

One roller-coasters to the ground,
becomes a verb people shoulder
in the past tense, becomes an
edge that no longer stretches.

BROOKLYN PASTOR SAYS HE AND HIS WIFE WERE ROBBED OF MORE THAN $1 MILLION IN JEWELRY WHILE PREACHING

CNN.com—July 25, 2022

It was a stellar split-screen moment shooting
straight from the tall-tale teeming Tropic of
Sir Lancelot or the lost psycho annals of
you'll-never-believe-this-total-bat-crazy-shit!

It's a line-turn in front of the congregation,
the pastor's baubles a prism bling-blinking,
the beacon more adorned than pearly gates.

This is a world catching up to gold.
The congregation's sound cacophony dances
past the stage. How they hear religion like
a trinket falling off a mic.

Then the gun-toting entrance no one will forget.
Pastor Miller-Whitehead's mind was glued
to a cross whose arms shook like wings,
how his face drained as thieves took his shine,
the wide-mouthed silence lapping the church pews,
plain spoken as negro spirituals.

TORONTO'S 2022 CARIBBEAN CARNIVAL PARADE DANCES BACK TO LIFE WITH JEWELLED HEADPIECES, FEATHERED WINGS—AND LOTS OF WATER

TORONTO STAR—JUL. 30, 2022

They lime ahead of the bandstand panyard
where they'll set musical jabs to gas-up judges
and set the days groove to a steelpan step.
Floats flow out the stadium like rolling fruit
from a cornucopia's soft hollow, the filled flat
trucks and wild mas revellers squawk like
flamingos and pelicans wining and gyrating
like legions of spiralling tops hand-scattered
through the vibe-full road stretch, their
multicoloured feathered crowns sway like
palm fronds in the afternoon's widening crest.
This is the world set to rhythm. The five kilo-
metre jump-trek bending to Sunnyside leans
endless hours to a blur, the rum ferris wheel
spinning upright in those who've taken mid-sun
on roadside split patches of crab grass.
It's the bright star return of a timeless
bloom no longer hidden under two years of
virus-plagued earth, now sprouting memories
again long after the day is stitched and gone.

BISHOP CHARGED IN SEXUAL ASSAULT AT BRAMPTON CHURCH

Welland Tribune—Aug. 12, 2022

Trust is what's splattered
at the rainbow's end when

the prism is layered
with cuts of light.

A woman tries to hold
the vision of a man she

can no longer see, pitch
darkness at the light's ledge.

Acknowledgements

Boundless gratitude to the Missouri Review for publishing "Ottawa police apologize for handling of incident after white woman calls 911 on Black man in a park" and designating it "Poem of the Week!"

Thanks to the following people for their advice, time, love, and support: Jean King, Karri Hutchinson, Al Moritz, Michael Callaghan, Gabriela Campos, Beatriz Hausner, Michael Mirolla, George Elliott Clarke, Myna Wallin, Molly Peacock, Krystyna Wesolowska, Barry Callaghan, James Deahl, Carol Morrison, Heather Wood, Rosemary Sadlier, David Clink, Kevin Pennant, Pablo Garcia, Fauzia Alarakhia, and Monique Twigg.

Ample and extensive thanks to the Toronto Arts Council, Ontario Arts Council, and the Canada Council for the Arts.

About the Author

Michael Fraser is published in *Best Canadian Poetry in English* 2013 and 2018. He has won numerous awards, including Freefall Magazine's 2014 and 2015 poetry contests, the 2016 CBC Poetry Prize, the 2018 Gwendolyn MacEwen Poetry Competition, and the League of Canadian Poets' 2022 Lesley Strutt Poetry Prize.

Printed by Imprimerie Gauvin
Gatineau, Québec